DEVELOPING SERVANT LEADERS

Developing Servant Leaders

Wayne Rautio

Copyright © 2022 by Wayne Rautio

All rights reserved. No part of this book may be reproduced in any manner whatsoever without written permission except in the case of brief quotations embodied in critical articles and reviews.

ISBN: 978-0-578-28062-2 (Paperback)

Scripture quotations, unless otherwise noted, are taken from The Holy Bible, New King James Version (NKJV). Copyright © 1982 by Thomas Nelson, Inc. Used by permission. All rights reserved.

First Printing, 2022
Second Printing, 2023 (revised edition)
Third Printing, 2024 (revised edition)

Contents

About the Author	vii

I
Leadership Basics   1

1	Introduction to Leadership	2
2	Basic Training	9
3	Planning & Decision Making	21
4	Stepping Out with God	37

II
Nuts & Bolts for Management   53

5	Ministry Health & Leadership Development	54
6	Internship & Mentoring Program	59
7	Challenges of Leadership	76
8	Out-of-the-Box Thinking	84

Appendix A – Additional Resources	89

About the Author

Wayne M. Rautio was born into a Finnish-American family in northern Michigan; his life consisted of hard work. In the summer, he played a lot of baseball, and in winter, ice hockey.

His hockey career was going really well until he had a very serious back injury and was paralyzed from his hips down. He had no feeling in his legs for about 2 to 3 months. He was told by the doctor that he would never play hockey again nor walk.

Well, Wayne proved him wrong, as he has done both ever since recovering a few months later.

After his hockey days, he went into construction in New England where he met his wife, Diane. As of this writing, they have been married for 56 years. They also have three (3) children and four (4) grandchildren.

In construction, he started developing people as he also did in sports. He trained many laborers, operators as well as supervisors. He had another back injury which led to surgery. After recovering from surgery, he left the construction industry and went into missions.

He and his family moved from New England to Florida to work full time at Bibletown Bible Conference. He injured his back for the second time, which meant another operation. This is when Wayne and his wife were called into Child Evangelism Fellowship (CEF) of Palm Beach County, Florida, a work they enjoyed very much and God was increasingly bringing more people into the work. Ministry in Palm Beach County was growing very fast.

After two years in Florida CEF, they received a call from Finland to work with the Finnish people. They spent four (4) years in Finland, where Wayne did a lot of printing. Their children went to the Finnish schools and really enjoyed their time in Finland.

After the four (4) years there, the Rautios moved to Germany and worked with the American military chaplains in many of the North Atlantic Treaty Organization (NATO) bases throughout Europe.

They returned to the United States because of health issues, as well as the schooling of their then teens. Wayne returned to work in construction in New Hampshire, at which time he continued developing people to be better laborers, equipment operators and supervisors. He was also very active in CEF of New Hampshire as a member of the CEF of New Hampshire state board and teaching CEF material in many churches, as well as in Russia and the Baltics during short-term missions' trips.

While still in the construction industry, he was able to be used by God to build into the lives of students at the Cru Bible College in Moscow and Minsk. On the trips to Russia, he would always stop in the Baltics to teach and encourage CEF workers in all those countries. This is where he did a lot of developing directors to become better leaders. He traveled to these countries from 1995 until 2013, every year or every other year. During those trips he would speak 50 to 65 times during a 4 to 5-week trip.

In 1998 Wayne & Diane moved to Northern Virginia to be the Executive Director of CEF of Northern Virginia. There was really no work to speak of when they arrived nor was there any money coming in. So, the first 5 to 7 years they lived on 25% of their salary. Wayne slowly started developing summer missionaries, and over the next 20 years, 10 young people developed into very good leaders. Several of these young people came back as many as 12 to 14 years to work with Wayne in the summer Christian Youth in Action (CYIA) program! It has only been in the past five years that he has seen the adults want to be trained as the young people were.

As more adults were trained in leadership, the staff grew to include three (3) full time staff, two (2) part time office workers, and three (3) part time coordinators overseeing the Good News Clubs (GNC). In 2019, CEF of Northern Virginia's goal was to have 60 active Good News Clubs reaching 2,000 children each week, and they achieved it!

Their new goal is 65 to 70 clubs, reaching over 2,500 each week. God is good.

We praise Him for all He has done and give Him all the honor and glory for what has been accomplished.

I

Leadership Basics

1

Introduction to Leadership

As you contemplate "Developing Servant Leaders", you are most likely saying, "What? Another book or series on Leadership?" I realize that there are many books written on this subject, but suggest that what is written here is a little different.

While the contents apply to all Christian workers, they are directed primarily towards those who are involved in any ministry or organization whose aim is to evangelize. Therefore, my aim is to help you in your ministry.

I believe some of you may be hesitant about reading this. You may think that you are not a leader, and you may not see yourself as providing leadership to others. You may, instead, feel that you are a follower, and are happy doing so.

I would like to point out several facts to all who have such reactions and reservations:

- Most Christians, all Christians, are leaders in some way. You may not see yourself as a great or gifted leader, but if you look closely at your life you'll realize that your words and/or actions influence someone! That is leadership in its most basic sense.
- Almost all of us are both leaders and followers. It is not a question of being one or the other. It is possible, and often

necessary, to be both. A full time Christian worker who works in a local area is looked upon as a leader by the teachers who attend his training class and by the young people who work as summer missionaries.

I want to emphasize that I don't see myself as an expert about leadership. I have written this because I feel that there are many Christian workers who need help in this area, to whom I may be able to give some guidance. And yet, I know that I, myself, am still in the learning process.

Much of what I have written has been culled from others whose books I have read or to whom I have listened. Indeed, so much helpful information has been gathered here and there through the years that I often don't know from where it came; thus, I am unable to pinpoint the source. But I have also included many lessons which I have learned or tried to learn (or failed to learn) during almost 50 years in a leadership position in Child Evangelism Fellowship. Most of my adult life has been in leadership and developing other people to become leaders, (sports, being in leadership positions in construction).

I trust that this series will help you to learn the lessons I have learned, to avoid some of the mistakes which I have made. My desire and prayer are to communicate to you how you can become one who can reproduce yourself successfully.

HOW LEADERSHIP ABILITIES CAN BE DEVELOPED

Are leaders born or made? Both.

- Some are born but still need to be made.
- Others are not born—and need to be made.

It should be pointed out, first, that leadership is one of the gifts of the Spirit. It is listed in Romans 12 v8 as "ruling", and in 1 Corinthians

12 v28 as "government" or "administration." A gift of the Spirit is a supernatural ability which God the Holy Spirit gives to an individual at, or after, conversion to help build the Church of Jesus Christ. In this way God has raised up some of the most unlikely people to be leaders and has blessed and used them in ministry. **But their ministry was based first, on an attitude of availability**; *then* God gave them the ability to lead.

In both cases the gift or ability needs to be developed. Timothy was exhorted not to neglect the gift that was in him (1 Timothy 4 v14), and encouraged to stir up the gift of God which was in him (2 Timothy 1 v6):

- **Ask** God to help you develop your leadership ability.
- **Use** your ability and not neglect it in any way.
- **Learn** what you can do to become a better leader.
- **Work** hard in the development process and put into practice what you have learned.
- **Be patient**. Transformation and progress take time; it does not happen overnight.

I want to share a brief look at the biblical plan for leadership, and to see how important leadership is in the purposes of God.

THE BIBLICAL STEPS FOR LEADERSHIP

When God calls a person into His service, be it in leadership or elsewhere, His plan for that ministry generally follows four steps:

- **VISION** - He/she needs to have four "visions" from the Word of God. These "visions" are not seen with the eyes but understood in his heart:
    - A vision of God and His Sovereignty
    - A vision of the person and his/her needs

- A vision of the Gospel and its power
- A vision of him/herself and his/her responsibility
- **VENTURE** - Act, obeying the vision which God has granted.
- **VALLEY** - Expect that there will be valleys—valleys of disappointment, discouragement, and even depression. But remember this vision or call and do not give up. Reflect on the character of God and have peace.
- **VICTORY** - Victory is the realization of the vision at some time in the future. But victory is also the ability to persevere in the present, and to enjoy the peace of God. It is joy in the journey!

These are the steps which all leaders have experienced whether they were leaders in the Bible, such as Abraham, Moses, Nehemiah, or Paul, or leaders in church and missionary history like William Carey, Hudson Taylor, Charles Spurgeon or C. T. Studd.

These four steps can be clearly seen in the ministry of Peter and in the development of his leadership:

- In Peter's life we can see a two-fold **vision.** The Lord Jesus showed him:
    - What he would **do** (Luke 5:8). He would become a fisher of men.
    - What he would **be** (John 1:42; Matthew 16:17-18). He would become a rock.

    Both seemed impossible at that time.

- Peter **ventured** all based on that vision (Luke 5:11; Mark 10:28).
- Peter experienced several **valleys.**
    - He was corrected by his Master (John 13:6-10).
    - He was rebuked by his Master (Matthew 16:23).
    - He had the wrong reactions (John 18:10-11).

- He fell asleep at the wrong time (Matthew 26:36-46).
- But the deepest valley of all was his denial of His Master (Matthew 26:69-75).

Although Peter was upset and even devastated by his failures, he did learn lessons from those failures which were to help in his later ministry. They would also help him in his writing the two letters which would become one of the most important parts of his ministry— for many centuries to come.

A leader who has made mistakes, *knows, and admits that he has,* is in a good position to help others to avoid making the same mistakes.

The Lord Jesus graciously restored him and led him onto the fourth step:

- **Victory** for Peter was the fulfillment of the **vision** outlined by the words of the Lord Jesus several years previously:
  - He "fished" for souls: 3,000 men (and women) on the Day of Pentecost were caught up into the kingdom of God (Acts 2:41).
  - He demonstrated his new stability and rock-like nature in his preaching, often before a hostile or indifferent audience (Acts 2:14-40; Acts 3:8-22; Acts 5:29-32); in his writing (1 Peter and 2 Peter), in his leadership and wisdom (Acts 5:3-4; Acts 10:9-48; and in his courage and fearlessness (Acts 12:3-19).

My prayer is that what I have written will be a help to each person who reads and does a serious study of this series. Also, this will result in a personal blessing for Christian workers, resulting in the salvation and spiritual growth of, "One more person, One more family, One more community".

I give all the Honor, Glory and Praise to my Lord and Savior Jesus Christ for allowing me to be able to be a servant for Him since my commitment to Him in 1967.

QUESTIONS:

1. Are You a leader?
2. Are you willing to learn to become a servant- leader?
3. Has God given you a vision to lead?
4. Are you working to develop that vision?
5. What was Apostle Peter's two-fold vision?

2

Basic Training

PERSONAL EXPERIENCE

The author states this session, "Developing Servant Leaders", to say that there are many books written and many different approaches that one can take, and perhaps get some results. His experience over the years has not come from such books, but from God's putting him in situations where he needed right-hand people to work with him, as mentioned in the "Introduction". He also gives credit to his father, who taught him a lot along these principles.

WHAT IS "LEADERSHIP"?

Most Christians, all Christians, are leaders in some way. You may not see yourself as a great or gifted leader, but if you look closely at your life, you'll realize that your words and/or actions influence someone! That is leadership in its most basic sense.

***Everyone* can *learn* to lead.**

WHAT ARE THE GOALS OF "LEADERSHIP"?

Maturity through Change – *Are you willing to change?*

The goal of developing leaders is "change," as in the lesson, "Teachers that Touch Lives." We must be willing to change to be a better leader and to develop others to become better leaders. Many leaders fail in this area because they are not willing to change. Others fail out of ignorance. Along with the session on "Teachers that Touch Lives" Mandatory teaching should be "The Victorious Life" textbook by J. Irvin Overholtzer. Strong complementary scripture passages are Proverbs 3:5-6 and Joshua 1:1-6.

These Resources are available from local CEF chapters or CEF Inc:

- "Teachers that Touch Lives," CEF Teacher Enrichment series
- "The Victorious Life" textbook by J. Irvin Overholtzer

Multiply Disciples – *Can you reach all the lost in your community by yourself?*

One should be willing to train 10 people rather than do the work of 10 people.

Patience and perseverance are requirements in one's ministry of influencing, guiding and leading others. But one can lead only those who are willing to follow.

Someone has said:

"An **effective** leader guides people and commands respect. He inspires them and exudes enthusiasm. An **ineffective** leader drives people and demands respect."

Another has said:

"A Christian leader can accomplish God's Will in, with, and through people to the Glory of God. He:

Must know God's Will

Accomplish God's Will in people
Accomplish God's Will with people
Accomplish God's Will through people."

When Peter speaks about the responsibility of leaders or elders, he emphasizes that their top priority is to *"feed the flock of God which is among you"* (1 Peter 5:2). The picture here is that of a shepherd and the main responsibility of a shepherd is to feed his sheep.

The shepherd fed his sheep – and he led them.

It has often been said that the main responsibility of a leader is not to devote himself to the work he does, but to devote himself to the workers who are accountable to him. His priority is to love them, help them and feed them. Personal interest, concern and counsel often is of greater value and benefit to them than just giving direction and can help in giving that direction. The work must not keep you from your workers.

We need to spend more time "feeding" and not just "leading."

Many of us think we are too busy to get involved in this way but, if we do, God will bless both the work and the worker in a special way and, as we care for them, they will in turn demonstrate their love and loyalty.

It is very important to listen to your workers, to talk to them, to help them, to advise them and to encourage them. Take time TO FEED THEM. The more you feed them, the better you will lead them.

THE CALLING

"Then he said to his disciples, "The harvest is plentiful, but the workers are few. Therefore, pray to the Lord of the harvest to send out workers into his harvest."" (Matthew 9:37-38, NKJV)

In developing leaders, just as in Missions, one must be called! You are being called into a Mission that is not your work, but *God's* work and God's work must be accomplished God's way or it will not prosper.

> *"Then I heard the voice of the Lord asking: "Who will I send? Who will go for us?"*
> *I said: "Here I am. Send me.""* Isaiah 6:8, NKJV

The call of God is for everyone! However, we need to be in tune with God to hear His call.

> *"He who calls you is faithful, who also will do it."* 1 Thessalonians 5:24, NKJV

THE TASK

The task in its simplest definition is to help train one other person in your area of the ministry.

THE PROCESS

APPROACH: One-on-One Mentoring

Are you a...	Mentor & Develop ...
Pastor	An Assistant Pastor
Sunday School Leader	An assistant/alternate Leader
Sunday School Teacher	Secondary Bible Teacher
Missions Director	An Assistant/Alternate Director
Music Director	An alternate Music Director
Administrator	An assistant Administrator
Nursery Coordinator	Alternate Coordinator(s)
Hospitality Coordinator	An assistant/alternate Coordinator
Missionary	A protégé or two

- *Experienced workers teach the inexperienced workers*

In my own life I have used this process in sports, construction (laborers, operators of machinery, and supervisors), and summer missionaries (I always had a right-hand young person who was my leader. This person would in turn, work on developing others). I used the same process to develop coordinators in CEF, who then developed assistants to be able to take over their jobs. The teacher must accomplish this as well; to have another able to step into the teacher's role at any time.

This is a long process.

At the director level, it is usually at least a two (2) to five (5) year or more process. The teacher must have leadership abilities and some success in the area that he/she is advising. The leader also must know that he/she is the leader and is actively training the person to eventually take his/her place.

Is the one in a leadership role mentoring other people to take his place or is he a one-man show? If he is a one-man show, he will not be able to develop another person to lead. Also, if the one being mentored has his own agenda and is unwilling to listen or change, that will not work, either.

I remember a missionary doctor sharing with me that help any one person, group or area one must sit where they sit, to listen and watch how they work, live, and do things in order to help them. **This is a very important first step for the leader to even be able to help the person wanting to be developed**.

METHOD: Progressive Responsibility

- **Teach the first step.**

In step one, give them small assignments at first. When they learn this step, increase the difficulty to the next level. In this process, the protégé is learning to start making independent decisions. Always give honest evaluations: this is where you can tell whether this person is really hearing what is being said.

- **Repeat and support until the person is comfortable.**

Train a person to learn step one until it is just like knowing the back of his hand. This process might be very short, or rather lengthy.

- **Know when to "let go" and allow the person to do it completely on his/her own.**

In training someone like this, the teacher must know when to let go and let the learner step out and do it on his/her own. Now he/she might not do it exactly as you do because of a different personality, ethnicity or will simply do it a little differently from you. *What you are looking for is the same result.*

- **Teach the next step, repeating the above method.**

However, do not go to step two until the protégé learns step one, very well. Then and only then, should step two be considered. This way the learner does not have to worry about step one anymore and can concentrate on step two.

- **Don't overload someone with tasks and responsibilities.**

Going back to when you were teaching "The Victorious Life", you are also sharing your life story, the good results along with the failures and hard struggles. It will benefit the protégé if you show the real you and not try to portray yourself as perfect (intentionally or unintentionally).

The teacher's most important job through this process is to continue encouraging the student and be very honest with him/her. Be very careful to not overload with too much in each step, or he/she will burn out early. **Work much on how to schedule prayer time, office work, family time and personal time away from the work**.

BURNOUT – SIGNS & COUNTERMEASURES

In scheduling, be aware of time demands, and abilities. Carelessness in this area will burn out a worker.

- **What are some of the signs of burnout?**
    - Start losing focus.
    - Start making bad decisions.
    - Attitude changes.
    - Become less effective in one or more areas:
        - Home life
        - Personal life, and
        - Work life are all affected,
        - So he/she is becoming less effective in all areas.
    - **How to Counteract Burnout**
        - Step back – Rest

A dear friend's pastor slowed his pace. Their church's budget increased over 1000% in three years!

- Schedule
    - Personal Time
    - Family Time
    - Rest
- Accountability Partner

○ It is necessary to find an accountability partner: an objective, honest, discreet person outside of your work with whom to meet regularly, say once a week, over a cup of coffee.

Jesus accomplished all God sent Him to do in a short time, yet there's no indication he ever rushed. Once again, "He who calls you is faithful…"

BIBLICAL LEADERSHIP

Biblical Leadership = Servanthood

A training program needs to be utilized that keeps going forward, building on the prior session(s).

The servant-attitude is critical. The following is taken from Wayne Rautio's paper on "Spiritual Leadership."

- The word "leader" is only used six (6) times in the Bible.
- The word "servant" is used repeatedly.
- Servant Leadership – exemplified by Jesus Christ.
    - Matthew 20:28 – *"just as the Son of Man did not come to be served, but to serve, and to give His life a ransom for many."* (NKJV)

Be Complete[1]

The Man or Woman of God must be Complete (2 Timothy 3:16-18). Two things are important in a Christian's life:

Character:

- **What you are**
- **What people sense you are**
  - Romans 8:28-29
  - God allows things to come into my life so that I may be more like the Lord Jesus. Stuart Briscoe has said, "Things have happened **TO** me, in order that things should happen **IN** me, so that things can happen **THROUGH** me." Frustrations are character-building – be careful that the right attitude is showing.
- **Attitudes**
  - **Christ-like attitudes**
  - Philippians 2:5-11
  - God is more concerned about our attitudes than our actions. If attitudes are right, actions will be right.

The mind of Christ did not elevate Him – it caused Him to be a servant. *His mind in us and through us should make us a servant.* Be careful that the right attitude is showing. People need to be attracted to us by the Christ-like life shining through us.

Leadership Building "Test" by R.E. Thompson

How we handle relationships tells a lot about our potential for leadership. R.E. Thompson suggests these tests:

- Do other people's failures *annoy* or *challenge* you?
- Do You *use* people, or *cultivate* people?
- Do you *direct* people, or *develop* people?
- Do you *criticize*, or *encourage*?

- Do you *shun,* or *seek out* the person with a special need or problem?

These tests mean little unless action is taken to correct them and fill the gaps in our training. The leader must be ready and able to teach. Maturity is when the root takes hold downward before it can bear fruit upward.

Rooted & Fruitful

Our maturity should be one where the root must take hold downward before it can bear fruit upward.

- *"... and if the root is holy, so are the branches."* Romans 11:16b (NKJV)
- *"... Yet he has no root and endures only for a little while. For when tribulation or persecution comes because of the word, immediately he falls away." Matthew 13:21 (NKJV)*
- *"... that you, being rooted and grounded in love, may be able to comprehend with all the saints what is the width and length and depth and height — to know the love of Christ which passes knowledge; that you may be filled with all the fullness of God."* Ephesians 3:17-19(NKJV)

Responsibilities of a Leader

If the World demands maturity as a standard of its leaders, the Church or Mission of the living God should select its leaders with even greater care.

- "To the elders among you; ...
    - Cast your care on Jesus – He cares for you (1 Peter 5:1-7)
    - Properly feed the "flock of God" (1 Peter 5:2)
    - Don't be dictatorial.
    - Be a worthy example (Titus 2:2; 1 Timothy 3:8, 11)

- Be a man or woman of prayer (1 Thessalonians 7:17)
- Be clothed "with humility" (1 Peter 5:5)

God's Promises

- *"He who calls you is faithful, who also will do it."* 1 Thessalonians 5:24 (NJKV)
- *"and when the Chief Shepherd appears, you will receive the crown of glory that does not fade away."* 1 Peter 5:4 (NKJV)
- Remember we are not alone in leadership.
  - *"...and lo, I am with you always, even to the end of the age.' Amen."* Matthew 28:20b (NKJV)
  - The burden should never be too heavy or too big because God cares for you. *Let worries go.*

"Also, I heard the voice of the Lord, saying: 'Whom shall I send,
And who will go for Us?'
Then I said, "Here am I! Send me."' Isaiah 6:8, NKJV

Endnote:

1. "Be Complete" section is from "The Christian Worker" lesson in the "Dynamics of Christian Leadership" series.

QUESTIONS:

1. How is leadership defined?
2. What is the importance of developing leaders?
3. What are some goals of leadership?
4. What is leadership?
5. Should there be a call?
6. How would you explain the process?
7. What are some signs of burnout?
8. How is burnout counteracted?
9. What is the difference between a leader and a servant-leader?
10. What two attributes are necessary for effectual leadership?
11. By what five points does R.E. Thompson test leader building?
12. Why is maturity required for a servant-leader?
13. What are the responsibilities of a leader?
14. Can you recite some of God's promises that a leader can claim?

3

Planning & Decision Making

"My son, do not forget my law, but let your heart keep my commands; ... Trust in the Lord with all your heart, and lean not on your own understanding; in all your ways acknowledge Him, and He shall direct your paths." Proverbs 3:1a, 5-6 (NKJV)

TWO WAYS TO LIVE

A choice must be made of two ways to live: either trusting God or leaning on our own understanding. This is a very important lesson to teach the children.

- **Follow God**
    - Not easy or automatic
    - *"Then Jesus said to His disciples, 'If anyone desires to come after Me, let him deny himself, and take up his cross, and follow Me.'"* Matthew 16:24 (NKJV)
- **Go Your Own Way**
    - Seems right, ... ends in death.

- *"There is a way that seems right to a man, but its end is the way of death."* Proverbs 14:12 (NKJV)

Studying the Book of Proverbs focuses on decision-making, one of the most important life skills one can develop, because we are blessed and burdened with an endless array of choices today from the petty to the profound.

An explosion of technology and communication over the past 20 years has multiplied our options exponentially. Now, instead of choosing among the local rock, country, hip-hop or classical radio stations you can choose among Spotify, Apple music or a podcast. Instead of choosing to watch what used to be the main TV channels each night, you may, on demand, view more content than you could ever consume in a lifetime.

Speaking of a lifetime, choices which shape our lives must be made that have little to do with technology. Which school should I attend? Which major should I pursue? Which job should I pursue? Which man or woman should I pursue, or should I let them pursue me? Should we really get married? Should I go back to work? Is it time to head in a new direction with my career? What should I do about my aging parents? What should I do about my adult children? For whom should I vote?

How is it all navigated? Is there some trick to decision-making, some hack that can be applied to reduce the stress associated with all these options? Yes, there is. It is found in a book that is thousands of years old, written to people living in a completely different context.

Remember, a father wrote proverbs to give his son instructions for life, including what to value and what to avoid. In other words: how to make good choices. Though we have more options than any other people living at any other time in history, certain foundational truths about life and meaning have never changed. The Book of Proverbs addresses those core principles and gives us a useful framework for planning and decision-making that still applies directly to our modern lives.

> *"My son, do not forget my law, but let your heart keep my commands; for length of days and long life and peace they will add to you."* Proverbs 3:1-2 (NKJV)

That's important to note – here's how to find peace:

> *"Let not mercy and truth forsake you; bind them around your neck, write them on the tablet of your heart, and so find favor and high esteem in the sight of God and man."*
> Proverbs 3:3-4 (NKJV)

Father says, "I'm telling you how to live in a way that honors God and gives you a good reputation in the sight of other men and women." And here's what it all comes down to:

> *"Trust in the Lord with all your heart, and do not rely on your own understanding [or don't depend or rely]; in all your ways know [submit to] him, and he will make your paths straight."*
> Proverbs 3:5-6 (ESV)

Proverbs 3:5-6 is one of those key passages of the Bible. These are verses heard again and again in your Christian life because the principle is so foundational: our lives should reflect faith and trust in God and His supremacy in all things. That is true whether in the Middle East 3,000 years ago or here in the western nations in the twenty-first century. The details of life may look different, but the foundational principle remains: Trust God and His supremacy in all things.

There are several points that we want to cover.

1. There are two ways to live – I can either follow God or go my own way.
2. Choosing to follow God is neither easy nor automatic.
3. Following God requires faith and trust in Him, as well as humility and discipline for me.

In summary, here are some practical steps you can take to discover God's direction for your life.

First, we see there are two ways to live – you can trust in the Lord with all your heart and accept His direction for your path, or you can lean on your own understanding. In other words, you can choose between what God commands and desires, or you can try to figure things out on your own. You can acknowledge God in all your ways, or you can ignore Him. It's a real struggle we face every day. And God isn't hiding it or ignoring it. Don't be shocked, or think you're special, when you have what seems like a new, different, or better idea about how to live – life has always been that way. Go all the way back to the garden of Eden and you'll discover Adam and Eve had their own ideas too – their own understanding of what would happen if they ate from the tree.

Unfortunately, contrary to what we want to believe – all roads don't lead to the same destination, not all opinions, ideas, and philosophies are true.

Later in the Book of Proverbs we find it put this way:

> *"There is a way that seems right to a man, but its end is the way of death."* Proverbs 14:12 (NKJV)

Now, I think we can all agree with that to some degree, we have all had the experience of thinking we were making a good choice, expecting it to go well, and then having things fall apart, break down, or blow up on us. We thought it was a good idea, but it turned out to be the wrong choice.

Often, what happens in those situations is that we were surprised by something we hadn't expected. There was a variable we didn't factor in and it affected the outcome.

And, of course, God is the largest variable of all. If you leave Him out of your planning, it can have catastrophic effects on your predictions.

But and here is our second point: choosing to acknowledge God and His direction for life is neither easy nor automatic. The call to trust, acknowledge and follow God is compelling speech; an imperative, an ultimatum. Why? Because this is not what we normally do.

Normally, we lean on our own understanding. Our default position is to operate independently, to make our decisions in a God-vacuum, even if we know Him.

When reading the Old Testament scriptures, you find Israel trusting in the walls they built around their cities for protection (Deuteronomy 28:52), or in political or military leaders they have chosen (Judges 9:26). Israel is forming coalitions and putting their trust in political alliances with surrounding nations (2 Kings 18:22 and others) or trusting in their wealth (Psalm 49:6; 52:70).

And these are people who knew God and experienced *prophets* and *miracles*. The Book of Proverbs is addressed to the son of King Solomon, the wisest man to ever live, a young man who grew up in Jerusalem, and saw the majestic temple right next to the palace. And yet, even he is told:

> *"Trust in the Lord with all your heart, and lean not on your own understanding"* Proverbs 3:5 (NKJV)

Friends, it is important to note there is a very real possibility, that even those of us who know God, and have experienced this work in our lives, can drift off course over time as new challenges come our way.

The Apostle Paul put it this way to the church of Galatia:

> *"Are you so foolish? Having begun in the Spirit, are you now being made perfect by the flesh?"* Galatians 3:3 (NKJV)

You started by receiving the mercy and blessings of God that he freely gave, and are you now trying to do things on your own, leaning on your own understanding? God has blessed you in the past, taken care of you, proven his love and mercy toward you, but now you're facing this. And this seems bigger, or more complex. It feels like there's more on the line, and you're looking around at other options, trying to figure things out instead of resting and trusting.

So, let's talk about that for a minute – let's bring some ugly stuff out of the shadows of our soul and into the spotlight and ask: "What are the things I am prone to trust in?"

We all have them. "As long as this or that is there, I'm fine.", "As long as he or she or they are involved, I'm fine.", or "As long as this or that happens, I'm fine." **But how many of us say, 'I'm trusting in the Lord with all my heart, so I know it's going to be fine'?**

BARRIERS TO FOLLOWING GOD

We want to have control.

Why don't more of us answer that way, or answer that way about more things?

In a word: control. We want to have control. We want guaranteed outcomes. It's hard to trust in the Lord, because He might not give me what I want. Or there might be a better way or a faster way or an easier way for me to get what I want than waiting patiently on God.

We have unrealistic expectations.

Sometimes we have unrealistic expectations. We expect things to work out perfectly and to always go well. We might not say it or think it this clearly, but most of us, even in the church, have an expectation that life should be rather easy, free of disasters and tragedies if you do it right.

But God says we live on a broken planet surrounded by sinful people. Sometimes we're going to experience the effects of that. Read scripture, study history, and you will find plenty of people, wonderful, holy, dedicated, and mature saints of God who suffered terrible tragedies in their lives, but still trusted God. Don't start leaning on your own understanding just because life isn't perfect. God never said it would be. That's why He's asking you to trust Him. If life was perfect, easy, and instantly fulfilling, it wouldn't require trust – you would live surrounded by proof and evidence.

Brothers and sisters, we require a near constant spiritual recalibration of our souls lest we too wander off, led by our own understanding, seeking outcomes we think we can control or influence or understand instead of acknowledging Him in all our ways and allowing Him to keep directing our paths.

One way to fight against this drift is to continue to communicate with God first thing in the morning before you communicate with anyone else. End your day acknowledging God and His place in your life, considering how that affects your place in this world.

Because there are two ways to live, choosing to acknowledge God, accepting His direction, and trusting Him is not always easy. This brings us to our third point: we're going to need to grow our faith and trust in God while humbling and disciplining ourselves.

We're told:

> "Trust in the Lord with all your heart ..." Proverbs 3:5 (NKJV)

But what does that mean? How is that done? Well, it's not all emotional. The idea of the heart here includes the inner self, the mind, will, heart, and understanding. Faith and trust are interwoven here. Both feelings and logic are involved.

In fact, the mind helps to motivate the heart, and the heart helps to moderate the mind. So I need to ask myself – do I really believe that God is God? Do I really believe that He is all knowing and therefore knows the best thing for me to do in a given situation? Do I really believe that He is kind and loving and therefore desires good for me in each situation? If so, I can trust Him.

And most likely we do, in some areas. We trust God to get us into heaven when we die. But do we trust Him with the details of tomorrow and this coming week? Often our trust breaks down because, instead of acknowledging Him in all our ways with all our heart, we acknowledge Him in some of our ways, with some of our heart.

Most of us want to be co-manager with God. We'll take some areas and let Him have others. But that's not all our heart, and that's not all our ways.

We're talking about the God who knows the end from the beginning; the God who tells how the earth and human history began and how it will end. This is the God who sits enthroned over all eternity, who has reigned forever and ever and will reign forever and ever more.

We want to understand first, then act

Instead of trusting Him, we are prone to lean on our own understanding.

How often do we make understanding a prerequisite to obedience? But it's not. There are many, many, things in life that you don't have to understand in order to obey.

- If you had to understand how a drug works, most of us could never take a prescription.
- If you had to understand how your phone works, you could never use it.

- If you had to understand how a plane flies, you could never take it.

So, why should understanding God precede trusting in Him? Mankind will always be prone to want to lean on his own understanding and own comprehension, instead of exercising faith and trust in God. So, at times, you will need to humble yourself, divest yourself of your own ideas, and even though you don't fully understand how it's all going to work out, step out in faith and obey.

> *"...in all your ways acknowledge him, and he shall direct your paths."* Proverbs 3:6 (NKJV)

Here we find a call to comprehensive, whole-life, Christian faith. There is no area of life that is outside of God's influence or direction. Acknowledge him in all your ways. God is not simply the God of Sundays and holidays and bad days. He is the God of everyday. God of the workplace and Good News Club, God of the sports fields, God over the kitchen, the basement and the bedroom, and God of the lecture hall and the lab.

Are you inviting God into all the areas of your life? Do you ask God for guidance and blessing at work? Do you seek Him as you think about scheduling the children's activities? Do you ask God to show you where to live, or what opportunities to take? Do you acknowledge Him in all of your ways?

Let's look at some very practical thoughts and ideas of what that may look like.

FOLLOWING GOD IN GENERAL

Sometimes God's directions are specific, but more frequently, His direction is general. Another way of saying this is: sometimes God's will is a dot and other times a circle. One can find His general will, the broad circle stuff, in His Word. The Bible never changes; it means the same thing to all people, at all times, in all cultures. A few examples include:

- **Salvation**

    "The Lord is not slack concerning His promise, as some count slackness, but is longsuffering toward us, not willing that any should perish but that all should come to repentance." 2 Peter 3:9 (NKJV)

- **Sanctification**

    "For this is the will of God, your sanctification: ..."
    1 Thessalonians 4:3a (NKJV)

- **Love One Another**

    "A new commandment I give to you, that you love one another; as I have loved you, that you also love one another. By this all will know that you are My disciples, if you have love for one another." John 13:34-35 (NKJV)

- **Wives, Submit to Your Husband - Husbands, Love Your Wife**

> *"Wives, submit to your own husbands, as to the Lord. "* Ephesians 5:22 (NKJV)
>
> *"Husbands, love your wives, just as Christ also loved the church and gave Himself for her,"* Ephesians 5:25 (NKJV)

The command, "husbands, love your wives like Christ loved the church" is an example of God's general direction. Expressions of a husband's love for his wife may vary from culture to culture and even from woman to woman. It doesn't mean all men, always, in all places, should bring their wives chocolates and flowers, but the general concept remains in play – no matter where you are, no matter how love is expressed culturally, husbands have an obligation to love their wives. That is God's general will.

FOLLOWING GOD IN SPECIFICS

God also provides specific direction for and in our lives. That is appealing. We like to know exactly what God wants us to do unless we disagree with it, but we usually like God's very specific, precise direction. Romans 12:2 provides a few examples of God's specific direction for our lives.

> *"... Do not be conformed to this world, but be transformed by the renewal of your mind, that by testing you may discern what is the will of God, what is good and acceptable and perfect."* Romans 12:2 (ESV)

God's specific will in our life-choices can be worked out as we consistently refuse to be conformed to this world, enable transformation of our spirit and character by renewing our mind with regular reading of God's word, and thereby also having the knowledge to discern or assess our decisions based on Biblical guidelines. For example, when a man is considering marriage, the Bible does not tell him specifically who he should marry. He can, however, assess the merits of his potential wife in accordance with Proverbs 31. A woman can also assess her own merits and character using Proverbs 31 as a standard.

The Bible also tells you to work hard, and describes work standards, but it does not tell you where to work. It tells you to love your neighbor, but it does not tell you where to live. In those areas, you are going to need to make specific applications of general principles. So here are some ways you can do that as you seek to acknowledge God and ask for his direction.

APPLICATION OF GENERAL PRINCIPLES

Check your motives.

It is important to check your own motives: Are you still leaning on your own understanding in some way? Are you trying to influence the outcome, or do you really, honestly, want whatever God says is best?

> *"Every way of man is right in his own eyes, but the Lord weighs hearts."* Proverbs 21:2 (NKJV)

Reach out to the Body of Christ

Second, reach out to the body of Christ. God has brought us into a family of believers – brothers and sisters who walk through life with us; He wants to use them to counsel and encourage us. In Proverbs King Solomon tells his son:

> *"I have taught you the way of wisdom; I have led you in right paths."* Proverbs 4:11 (NKJV)

Again, in Proverbs we read:

> *"Finalize plans with counsel, and wage war with sound guidance."* Proverbs 20:18 (NKJV)
>
> *"Without counsel, plans go awry, but in the multitude of counselors they are established."* Proverbs 15:22 (NKJV)

Ask other Christians for their thoughts and guidance and prayerfully consider their input

Look at circumstances.

Third, look at circumstances:

> *"A man's heart plans his way, but the Lord directs his steps."* Proverbs 16:9 (NKJV)

Is God opening or closing unexpected doors in front of you? If you lean on your own understanding, you are likely leaning on your own resources, too. However, God may have things you do not see and wants to use them to bring better outcomes for your situation. If you acknowledge Him and seek His direction, He may ask you to trust Him and lead you to do something you wouldn't have thought of or chosen on your own, because He's not going to leave you on your own – He's going to supply some surprises that change the final outcome!

But sometimes, you and I do not want to trust God because we are afraid that we will be wrong. If that is what is holding you back, you need to know this: God judges motives more than outcomes. If you're wrong, if you make a mistake, God always has the divine ability to step in and keep you from falling off the edge. But more often than not we do not get in trouble by trusting God; we get in trouble by leaning on our own understanding and making compromises to "make things work." The apostle Paul put it this way, writing to early Christians living in Rome:

> "*I beseech you therefore, brethren, by the mercies of God, that you present your bodies a living sacrifice, holy acceptable to God which is your reasonable service. And do not be conformed to this world, but be transformed by the renewing of your mind, so that you may prove what is that good, and acceptable and perfect will of God.*" Romans 12:1-2 (NKJV)

The Christian life is meant to be a response. We direct our lives toward God because of all He has already done for us. We were wandering, lost, perhaps ignorant or perhaps intentionally rebellious, but we were living for ourselves, leaning on our own understanding, following a path that seemed good to us, but which ends in destruction. Therefore, He interrupted our lives, or plan, brought us conviction, and offered us forgiveness in Christ and a new life – one meant to be lived with his guidance and direction and all the blessings – immediate and eternal that come from that.

Christians, *"[we have] been crucified with Christ, and [we] no longer live, but Christ lives in [us]. The life [we] now live in the body, [we] live by faith in the Son of God, who loved [us] and gave himself for [us]."* Galatians 2:20 (NKJV)

In light of all He has done for us, let us trust Him with all our heart today. In addition, teach the boys and girls how to acknowledge Him in all their ways.

Note:

Sermon by Pastor Jeff Schlenz, The City Gates Church, used by permission.

QUESTIONS:

1. What are the two ways to live?
2. What barrier(s) are there to following God?
3. What are the ways everyone needs to follow God? (His general will)
4. How does one follow in specifics?
5. What are applications of general principles?

4

Stepping Out with God

"For whatever things were written before were written for our learning, that we through the patience and comfort of the Scriptures might have hope."
~Romans 15:4 (NKJV)

While studying the Old Testament, anticipate a time of learning – to keep persevering, to comfort and encourage us, that we might have hope – a confident expectation about the future.

In reading Joshua 1:1-9, we are shown two factors in the process of stepping out with God:

1. God Communicates with His servants.
2. God Commands His servants.

STEPPING OUT WITH GOD - SERVING THE LORD

One Step at a Time

In serving the Lord, take one step at a time and persevere in the power of the Spirit. We sometimes get to the point: "I can't do this anymore." Then comes a new level of trust.

Obey the prompting of the Spirit

This next step could be a small step or maybe it is a big step – a major transition – a big change. Fear sets in, we need to pray and ask others to pray, we need to do some thinking, planning, but it is time to act. Obey the prompting of the Spirit – a little step of obedience.

GOD COMMUNICATES WITH HIS SERVANTS

Servants of the Lord *must hear* from the Lord! Look at Joshua 1:1 *"...the Lord spoke to Joshua..."* (NKJV) God spoke to Joshua and told him:

- **"Moses, my servant, is dead."** – *Leave the past behind.*

Joshua

Joshua had served as Moses' assistant for about forty years. For Joshua, this meant that his beloved mentor was gone. Moses was the spiritual leader whom he had grown to know and love, a man who modeled humble leadership, a man to whom Joshua looked for direction and who had shouldered the burden of responsibility and leadership for forty years.

The Apostle Paul

The Apostle Paul also learned to leave the past behind. Paul was full of religious zeal, and academic accomplishment, very self-confident, relying on his own gifts and abilities. He was at the top of his class and religious order, self-righteous, and blameless (in the eyes of Jewish law) and focused on zealously persecuting Christians. His meeting with Jesus Christ, on the road to Damascus, changed everything.

- *"Saul, Saul, why are you persecuting me?"* Acts 9:4; Acts 22:7 (NKJV) – **Leave the past behind.**
- *"Depart, for I will send you far from here to the Gentiles."* Acts 22:21 (NKJV) – **A time to step out.**

After a face-to-face meeting with the risen Savior, his life focused on knowing Christ, His power, and His sufferings.

> *"Brethren, I do not count myself to have apprehended; but one thing I do, forgetting those things which are behind and reaching forward to those things that are ahead, I press toward the goal for the prize of the upward call of God in Christ Jesus"* Philippians 3:13-14 (NKJV)

- *"Arise and go over this Jordan"* Joshua 1:2 (NKJV) – **A time to step out.**

This was a time for action after 40 years of wandering; after a 40-year delay, waiting for the older unbelieving generation to die.

THEN – 40 years prior, twelve leaders were sent by Moses to spy out the 'land flowing with milk and honey.' They returned with a cluster of grapes carried on a pole between two men. But they also reported that the cities were fortified, the people were strong and very large, sons of Anak. They were giants, and 'we looked like grasshoppers in our own eyes.' Ten of the twelve spies said, "We are not able to go against the people. They are stronger than we."

Caleb and Joshua were among the twelve spies and disagreed – "We shall overcome:"

> *"If the Lord delights in us, then He will bring us into this land and give it to us, a land which flows with milk and honey. Only do not rebel against the Lord, nor fear the people of the land, for they are our bread; their protection has departed from them, and the Lord is with us. Do not fear them."*
> Numbers 14:8-9 (NKJV)

And all the congregation threatened to stone them. Refer to Numbers 14:10.

NOW – It was time to trust God and step out. The giants were still there, the cities fortified to the sky, and the entrenched pagan nations are still there.

Is God giving you another chance to trust Him, step out in faith? In your past you said "no." Now there is another opportunity before you!

Joshua was to take all the people – about 2.5 million people by some estimates, a large undertaking – into the Promised Land. The people who were obstinate, complaining, grumbling, rebelling, disobedient and unbelieving people.

To Possess the Promise

- **God was already giving them the Land.**

This call to Joshua was a call to join God in what He was doing for his chosen people. It was not about Joshua.

> *"If anyone serves me, let him follow me; and where I am, there my servant will be also. If anyone serves me, him will My Father honor."* John 12:26 (NKJV)

God is working in our world. He invites us to join Him in what He is doing in the lives of people, including children – it is not about you or me.

Here, with Joshua, God is keeping his promise to Abraham, Isaac, and Jacob. 400 years have come and gone since God told Jacob to go down to Egypt. Unbelief meant delay, but now God is ready – it is time His people go into the Promised Land. Joshua is His instrument through whom God will keep working His redemptive plan.

Later in Israel's history, a man named David was God's instrument:

> *"... For David, after serving his own generation by the will of God..."* Acts 13:36 (NKJV)

There are multiple avenues for serving the Lord. It will mean serving for the good of others.

- **"Every place your feet tread"**

God told Joshua...

> *"Every place that the sole of your foot will tread upon I have given you, as I said to Moses."* Joshua 1:3 (NKJV)

God would keep His promise, but Joshua had to step out, walk, act in obedience and faith. God empowered Joshua to take possession of the promise and He will empower you to fulfill His calling in your life.

> *"His divine power has given us all things that pertain to life and godliness, through the knowledge of Him who called us by glory and virtue, by which have been given to us exceedingly great and precious promises, that through these you may be partakers of the divine nature, having escaped the corruption that is in the world through lust. But also, for this reason, giving all diligence, add to your faith virtue, to virtue knowledge, to knowledge self-control, to self-control perseverance, to perseverance godliness, to godliness brotherly kindness, and to brotherly kindness love."* 2 Peter 1:3-7 (NKJV)

Joshua had to take the next step; as he looked at what lay ahead, he saw that it would be a "big walk" because the land was large (see verse 4), and taking this territory was going to be a long, hard journey. There were the Amalekites in the south; Hittites, Jebusites, and Amorites dwelling in the mountains; and Canaanites dwelling by the sea and along the banks of the Jordan. They were "entrenched" – it would be difficult to remove them. But Joshua had faith in God's promises:

> *"No man shall be able to stand before you all the days of your life; as I was with Moses, so I will be with you. I will not leave you nor forsake you."* Joshua 1:5 (NKJV)

God's personal promise to Joshua

- Joshua did not need to fear the giants nor all those nations. God promised him that:
    - No man would be able to stand before him
    - God was with him
    - God would never leave or abandon him

What about you? Are you afraid to work with children, teenagers, or train a co-worker? If God moves you to work with a certain group of people, He will give you a love for those people. He also gives promises to mitigate the fear.

With the call to step out, God reminded Joshua:

- *"I will be with you, just as I was with Moses."*
- Joshua had been Moses' assistant for forty years and had seen or heard of the ways in which God had been with Moses:
    - As an infant – God protected him in the Nile River
    - In his formative years – God provided him with the best education that Egypt had to offer, as the Princess's foster son.
    - As an adult – Moses murdered an overseer, which resulted in his fleeing to the desert. Yet, while in the desert God provided a wife, children, and a profession for him while he was there.
    - Moses' return to Egypt – God was with him as he confronted Pharaoh.
    - During the exodus – God parted the Red Sea for Moses and the Israelites.
    - Wilderness wanderings – God provided water, food, and their shoes did not wear out.
- *"I will not leave you or abandon you."*
    - God will not leave you – His presence will be with you.
    - God will not abandon you – He will not "let go" of you.

> "Fear not, for I am with you; be not dismayed, for I am your God. I will strengthen you; I will help you. Yes, I will help you; I will uphold you with My righteous right hand." Isaiah 41:10 (NKJV)

> "So we may boldly say, 'The Lord is my helper; I will not fear. What can man do to me?'" Hebrews 13:6 (NKJV)

> "I give them eternal life, and they shall never perish; neither shall anyone snatch them out of my hand." John 10:28 (NKJV)

TYPICAL METHODS OF COMMUNICATION

Now that we've seen how God communicated with his servant Joshua, how does God communicate with his servants today? The three most typical methods of communicating include:

- Through Scripture
- Through Godly Counsel
- Through Circumstances

GOD COMMANDS HIS SERVANTS

After God has communicated with his servant, he also commands them.

"Be strong and of good courage"
- For the task
- For full obedience

God commanded Joshua, in Joshua 1:6-8, to:

"Be strong and of good courage" - *For the Task*

Joshua had a big task and responsibility put before him. *"... for you [Joshua] will divide as an inheritance the land I swore to their fathers to give them."* (NKJV)

He was commanded to be "strong"

- To devote himself to the task.
- Set his heart on it.
- To "go for it."

He was also commanded to be "of good courage."

- To be bold,
- Assured, and
- Confident

God chose Joshua for a particular task, at a particular time in redemptive history. It's interesting to note that prior to commanding Joshua, God had communicated and commanded Moses to "pass the torch" on to Joshua AND encourage him and strengthen him for the task.

> *"But command Joshua and encourage him and strengthen him; for he shall go over before this people, and he shall cause them to inherit the land which you will see."* Deuteronomy 3:28 (NKJV)

- **Kings David and Solomon's Example**

In Chronicles, chapter 28, we have a similar example. King David had wanted to build the Lord's Temple in Jerusalem, but God had told him, "No." However, God had conveyed the detailed plans for the building and staffing of the Temple to David. God wanted David's son Solomon to build the Temple. When the time came, God prompted King David to "pass the torch" on to his son Solomon with support and encouragement. David had made detailed and comprehensive preparations for building the Temple, all of which he passed on to his son along with encouragement:

> *"And David said to his son Solomon, "Be strong and of good courage, and do it; do not fear nor be dismayed, for the Lord God - my God - will be with you. He will not leave you nor forsake you, until you have finished all the work for the service of the house of the Lord."* 1 Chronicles 28:20 (NKJV)

Do you need to hear God say: "You are going to finish; finish the work, the task, the project that I have given you"?

"Only be strong and very courageous" - For Full Obedience

Joshua was to be strong and very courageous in observing ALL of God's law. He was to be fully obedient, not just partially obedient.

Are you living obediently in many areas, but resisting or ignoring the work of the Holy Spirit in other areas? Is there one area in your life you know is not pleasing the Lord? One area where God is prompting obedience? How are we going to observe all of God's law and to do all of God's work?

> *"... do not turn from it to the right hand or to the left, so that you may prosper wherever you go."* Joshua 1:7b (NKJV)

Stay focused on God's Word and the task he has set before you, not the task he has set before someone else. Your task. Is something distracting you from reading scripture? Or, from the task he has set before you?

> *"Do not love the world or the things in the world. If anyone loves the world, the love of the Father is not in him. For All that is in the world - the lust of the flesh, the lust of the eyes, and the pride of life - is not of the Father, but is of the world. And the world is passing away, and the lust of it; but he who does the will of God abides forever."* 1 John 2:15-17 (NKJV)

So, how do we focus on God's Word and the task He has set before us?

> *"This Book of the Law must not depart from your mouth; but you shall meditate in it day and night, that you may observe to do all that is written in it. For then you will make your way prosperous, and then you will have good success."* Joshua 1:8 (NKJV)

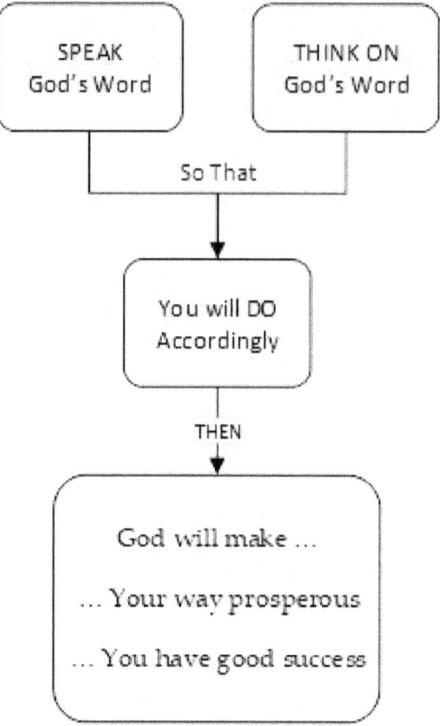

Figure 1: The process of obedience

And lastly, *"Have I not commanded you? Be strong and of good courage; do not be afraid, nor be dismayed, for the Lord your God is with you wherever you go."* Joshua 1:9 (NKJV)

- Say "No" to fear and dismay
- Do not be afraid – tremble: to be fainthearted
- Do not be dismayed – broken, shattered
- **"For the Lord your God is with you wherever you go."**

CHALLENGE

I challenge you to join the saints throughout the ages in stepping out with God! God said to these saints of old, "Go!"...

- **Abram / Abraham** – Go from your country and your kindred and your father's house to the land that I will show you. (Genesis 12:1)
- **Jacob** – Go to Egypt. Do not be afraid to go. (Genesis 46:3)
- **Moses** – Go to Pharaoh, "...that you may bring My people, the children of Israel, out of Egypt." (Exodus 3:10, NKJV)
- **Joshua** – Go, cross the Jordan, "...for you shall cause this people to inherit the land that I swore to their fathers to give them." (Joshua 1:1-6, NKJV)
- **Isaiah** – Go, "and say to this people." (Isaiah 6:9, NKJV)
- **Jeremiah** – Go, "I appointed you a prophet to the nations." (Jeremiah 1:4-8, NKJV)
- **Gabriel** – Go, tell Mary, "...you will conceive...and bear a son... call him Jesus." (Luke 1:26-33, NKJV)
- **Joseph** – Go, "take Mary to be your wife." (Matthew 1:20, NKJV)
- **Disciples** – Go, make disciples of all the nations (Matthew 28:16-20)
- **Ananias** – Go, heal Saul's eyes (despite the fact that Saul/Paul had done much harm to the saints; Acts 9:10-12)
- **Saul/Paul** – Go, to the Gentiles. (Acts 9:15; 22:12-16)
- Many others throughout history....
- God the Father, Son, and Holy Spirit on the threshold of Heaven –
  - **The Father said to His Son** – Go, save the lost.

"For God did not send his Son into the world to condemn the world, but that the world through him might be saved." John 3:17 (NKJV)

Your turn: Take your first step, then another step, take that big step.

Note:
Sermon by Vic Ransom, Fairfax County Detention Center Chaplain, given at The City Gates Church, used by permission.

QUESTIONS:

1. How does one serve God?
2. How did God communicate with His servants?
3. How did Joshua know to possess the promise?
4. What are some typical methods of communication?
5. What are some highlights in this chapter?
6. How did God command His servants?
7. Do we need to be afraid or dismayed?
8. Recall how each of the saints of old responded specifically to the command to go:
    a. Abraham - Genesis 12:1
    b. Jacob – Genesis 46:3
    c. Moses – Exodus 3:10
    d. Joshua – Joshua 1:1-6
    e. Isaiah – Isaiah 6:9
    f. Jeremiah – Jeremiah 1:4-8
    g. Gabriel – Luke 1:26-33
    h. Joseph – Matthew 1:20
    i. Ananias – Acts 9:10-12
    j. Saul/Paul – Acts 9:15; 22:12-16
    k. the Disciples – Matthew 28:16-20
9. Name one person not mentioned in the Bible who received a "Go!" from the Lord and describe what that entailed.

II

Nuts & Bolts for Management

The following section is intended primarily for Pastors, Directors and functional Leads. It provides guidelines for developing a systematic approach to developing leaders within a given functional or geographic area.

5

Ministry Health & Leadership Development

First, it is highly recommended that everyone, at all levels of involvement, in each ministry area go through the "Basic Training" session in "Developing Servant Leaders" training. This will help everyone "get on the same page," so to speak. While it's certainly not nearly as extensive as military boot camp, it is similar in its purpose – learn the ministry specific terminology and understand the main goals of the ministry. It will also facilitate team participation in developing a long-term plan for the area.

DEVELOP A 2-5-YEAR PLAN TO BUILD UP KEY AREAS OF THE MINISTRY.

Why develop a 2-5-year plan? *To ensure continuity for the long term.* Assess, prioritize, and have target training blocks *for leaders who can propagate the plan.*

Assess your area's needs

- Evaluate the spiritual condition of your co-workers as well as their ministry skills.
- Ask your co-workers what areas in which they feel they need more help or training.

Prioritize needs

- Prioritize training based on your evaluation and feedback from your co-workers.
- Identify what 2-3 areas of ministry that you, as a team, feel called to build.

You do not want to do the work of 10 men or women – get 10 men and women to do the work, starting with one at a time.

DEVELOP LEADERSHIP TRAINING "BLOCKS"

- Develop a series of leadership training "blocks"
    - For example: 2-Year multi-track Training Plan
- Cycle through training "blocks" with each area
    - Prioritize topics based on the needs assessment.
    - Include workshop sessions for practical skill(s) training.
    - Sample Training Plan

Developing Leaders
Training Plan
by Wayne Rautio

Year 1

General Sessions:

#	Title	Est. Time
Ph1 S1	Developing Leaders: Basic Training	60 min
Ph1 S2	Developing Leaders: Planning and Decision Making (Proverbs 3)	

Track 1 - Directors

#	Title	Est. Time
Ph1 S3	Developing Leaders: Ministry Health & Leadership Development	60 min
D-02	Workshop	

Track 2 - CEF Workers

#	Title	Est. Time
W-01	Teacher's That Touch Lives	60 min
W-02	Workshop	

Ongoing Training (Local Staff)

	Dynamics of Christian Leadership			The Victorious Life	
Oct	OTD-01	The Christian Worker		OTW-01	God's Provision
				OTW-02	God's Promises
Nov	OTD-02	Qualities of an Effective Leader		OTW-03	God's Presence
				OTW-04	God's Principles
Dec	OTD-03	Importance of Example in Leadership		OTW-05	God's Power
Jan	OTD-04	Cost of Leadership		OTW-06	God's Possession
Feb	OTD-05	The Servant Leader		OTW-07	God's Plan
	OTD-06	Learning to Lead in Love			
Mar	OTD-07	Motivating Your Workers		OTW-08	God's Protection
				OTW-09	The Victorious Life and Its Dangers
Apr	OTD-08	Recruiting and Leading Volunteers		OTW-10	The Glories of the Victorious Life
	OTD-09	Working With a Team			

OTD - Ongoing Training (Director level)
OTW - Ongoing Training (Worker level)

Updated: 2 Dec 2020

Figure 2: Sample Training Plan

- Workshops
    - Develop topic specific workshops to provide practical skill training. The workshops should complement existing written guidelines with a systematic walk-through of a specific task. They should also provide a few examples of how to apply the guidelines in various situations. Limit each session to 45-60 minutes in length. In some cases, the session may be shorter. Also, consider videotaping the workshop to post online for later reference (optional).
- Remember to Involve Your People
    - There are many roles and tasks that need doing within a given ministry opportunity. A well-oiled organization will cross-train its members and make sure each person has a backup in case of emergencies.

Are you a …	Mentor & Develop …
Pastor	An Assistant Pastor
Sunday School Leader	An assistant/alternate Leader
Sunday School Teacher	Secondary Bible Teacher
Missions Director	An Assistant/Alternate Director
Music Director	An alternate Music Director
Administrator	An assistant Administrator
Nursery Coordinator	Alternate Coordinator(s)
Hospitality Coordinator	An assistant/alternate Coordinator
Missionary	A protégé or two

IN CLOSING & ADDITIONAL RESOURCES

You want to motivate, not manipulate. Lasting motivation comes from within. A few potential topics to address with co-workers and provide training on include:

- Inward Motivation
- Character Development
- Leadership Training

QUESTION:

1. What are the three key areas on which to focus?

6

Internship & Mentoring Program

Natural leadership qualities all too often lie dormant and undiscovered. If we look carefully, we should be able to detect leadership potential. Moreover, if we have it, we should develop it and use it for Christ's work. Internships and mentoring programs are for leaders, those who want to become leaders, and those who want to develop others to become leaders – servant leaders.

CASE STUDY - CHRISTIAN YOUTH IN ACTION (CYIA), CEF OF NORTHERN VIRGINIA

Every year in CEF of Northern Virginia, Wayne Rautio had a right-hand person who was a Summer Missionary. When he saw some leadership qualities in one of the summer missionaries, he would start pouring his life into that young person. He started by giving him or her small assignments and then evaluated how they handle them. If they did well, he would keep giving them more and more responsibility until they became his right-hand person in the CYIA program. He then allowed them to begin teaching other summer missionaries. Wayne spent most of his time with the CYIA leader(s) of the teens, who in turn trained the remaining CYIA teens.

From the very first year that Wayne was in CEF of Northern Virginia (and that was over 20 years ago) he had a young person who was his CYIA leader. Some worked with him for 5 to 6 years and some worked with him for over 12 years. Here is one testimony of how God is using leadership training in the CYIA program:

> *The first time that Mr. Wayne came to speak at my church was around when I was 12 years old. I remember sitting near the front of the congregation, and was intrigued by his style of preaching. He didn't stand behind the podium the entire time, but walked back and forth on the stage to maintain eye contact with various congregation members. He then whipped out "stop" and "go" signs, and went over a song. This segued into his portion on Child Evangelism Fellowship, and the work that young people (and by young, he didn't mean young adult, but teens such as me at that time) had done for the children. I've always wanted to teach in Sunday School, but I was considered too young by my church leaders. I remember approaching Mr. Wayne after the service to learn more and quite frankly, ready to sign up and start. This was out of character for my 12-year-old self, I had always preferred to do things that were considered comfortable to me. Volunteering to meet new people and to speak in public was completely out of my comfort zone. But I did it. Little did I know how much of an impact that this ministry and the leadership/ mentorship that Mr. Wayne offered would have on my life.*
>
> *I had always been a fly on the wall. Teachers usually remembered me as the child who was shy, quiet, and did what she was told – nothing quite memorable. I joined CYIA with the intention to fly under the radar, and the hope to create some fond memories while working with children. To my surprise, Mr. Wayne saw this fly on the wall and reached out as a leader, a mentor, and most importantly, a friend. He never exerted his years of experience or the fact that he was the director of our group to demand respect.*

He showed us what it meant to be a child of God, and how that reflects in how we act and spoke to others, especially to the children. He helped me build my confidence but also was quick to ensure that I remained humble. All that we did was not for our own glory, not for all the praises we received from man, but for the glory of God.

As I continued to gain confidence in public speaking, Mr. Wayne began directing me to more leadership roles. His method in creating new leaders, wasn't simply putting you in the spot without training. It's through years of working with him, he begins to give little nuggets of opportunities to see how you will react and respond. He doesn't swoop in immediately to "fix it," but to allow you to make mistakes and grow. I didn't realize how much of an impact in how he grew leaders would have on me, until I had opportunities to be a mentor to others outside of CYIA. Many of the methods I used were in direct correlation to what Mr. Wayne did with me.

I am forever grateful for everything that Mr. Wayne has had in my life. He helped strengthen my faith and helped shape my perspective in life. His tremendous ability to be empathetic has helped him be able to connect to others, such as myself.

SERVANT LEADERSHIP

So where to start in developing leaders as in the case study above? God wants to show how strong He really is, and the Church today needs young men and women of God who will step up and be counted. Also, realize that it is God, alone, who appoints leaders. That is a wonderful thought!

We also need to heed the warning that if the leaders fail to guide their people towards the spiritual uplands, then surely the path to the lowlands will be well worn. People travel together; no one lives alone.

"... whoever desires to become great among you will be your servant, and whoever of you desires to be first shall be slave of all." Mark 10:43-44 (NKJV)

Requires Continual Change

To become a servant-leader, one needs to be willing to change, as discussed in Part 1. One who is unwilling to change will have a hard time becoming the servant-leader whom God wants.

Requires Humility

If you are of the mind-set that you do not need to change, I would recommend that you get on your knees now and ask God to change you. "What more do I have to learn?" has been uttered by so many people, and most of them never developed to become a leader, let alone a servant-leader. If you cannot yield a point when someone else's ideas are better, spare yourself the frustration of failing in leadership.

Comes with a Cost

"But Jesus said to them, 'You do not know what you ask. Are you able to drink the cup that I drink, and be baptized with the baptism that I am baptized with?'" Mark 10:38 (NKJV)

The suffering of spiritual leadership – there was no beating around the bush here. Jesus simply and honestly set forth the cost of serving in His Kingdom. There will be a cost in leadership.

LEADERSHIP BUILDING "TESTS"

How we handle relationships tells a lot about our potential for leadership. R.E. Thompson suggests these tests:

- Do other people's failures **annoy** or **challenge** you?
    - Don't Expect Perfection in yourself or others – We all need to learn by doing, by practice.
- Do you *"use"* people, or **cultivate** people?
    - Keep Confidences - If you cannot keep a confidence, do not try to lead.
- Do you **direct** people, or **develop** people?
    - Be Ready to Teach - The leader must be ready and able to teach. This is what I enjoy, even though many times I feel that I cannot do it; the Holy Spirit shows me repeatedly that He can and will, lead.
- Do you **criticize** or **encourage**?
- Do you **shun** or **seek out** the person with a special need or problem?

These tests mean little unless we act to correct them and fill the gaps in our training. Remember, we are not alone in leadership. *"Casting all your cares on him, because he cares about you."* 1 Peter 5:7. The burden should never be too heavy or too big, because God cares for you.

THE GOALS OF DEVELOPING LEADERS

- Maturity through Change
    - *Are you willing to change?*
- Multiply Disciples
    - *Can you reach all the children in your community by yourself?*
- Reach One more Person, One more Family, One more Community

- Is it worth your time and effort?

LEADERSHIP IS DEVELOPED

So where does one start with developing other leaders?

Gain First-Hand Experience

- **Learn before you teach**

One needs to gain experience in the field where he/she will be developing leaders. Otherwise, how can anyone show another what to do without previous experience? Here is where we need to have a highly competent person who trains others to become leaders.

Too many times people have been placed in charge in organizations, with absolutely no experience. How can that individual become successful in that area? One needs to have certain schooling and subsequent training under an experienced mentor to become the leader that the organization wants.

- **Position ≠ Leadership**
- **Advanced Degrees ≠ Leadership**

It is not always how many degrees a person has who should be placed in charge. Education is necessary, yet education for its own sake is useless unless practiced and applied in the proper setting.

"But be doers of the word and not hearers only ..." James 1:22 (NKJV) applies to secular as well as spiritual arenas.

It is not the amassing of education that God is looking for, although that can certainly be a plus, God is looking for a person who is CALLED to reach the lost. God doesn't necessarily call the equipped, but always equips the called. A "Calling" is very important – we will look at this in more detail later in the session.

Participate in an Internship / Mentoring Program

Participating in an internship or mentoring program can be a rewarding experience for:

- Personal Growth
- Acquiring Practical Skills

INTERNSHIP & MENTORING PROGRAMS

While internships are a form of mentoring program, there are differences between the two:

INTERNSHIP	MENTORING PROGRAM
Typically, a formal program	Typically, informal program
Includes written assessments	No written assessments
"On the Job Training (OJT)"	Train as you work & do life together

Leaders at all levels can mentor others. In addition to personal growth, internships and mentoring programs are necessary for growing the ministry and "working yourself out of a job."

"... *one who waters will himself be watered.*" Proverbs 11:25 (ESV)

PERSONAL LEADERSHIP DEVELOPMENT PLAN

Regarding "Personal Growth," especially those who are or want to become leaders, we need to ask ourselves if we are characterized by a proud or humble spirit. Moses' response to the rebellion of Korah teaches how to respond to any criticism. Numbers 16:1-3 describes the cause of criticism many leaders including Korah charge that Moses and Aaron take too much authority for themselves in view of the fact that all the congregation are holy. Though it was true that all the congregation was holy, they failed to recognize that Moses and Aaron were God-appointed leaders. Numbers 16:4 describes Moses' humble spirit: "When Moses heard this, he fell facedown." Moses was deeply wounded but he said nothing to vindicate himself. His main concern was God's glory, not his own position or privilege. I believe this should be our concern as well.

The following table will help us identify areas to work on in developing humble, servant-leader characteristics.[1]

PROUD SPIRIT	BROKEN, HUMBLE SPIRIT
Focuses on failures of others	Overwhelmed with sense of their own spiritual need
Self-righteous, critical, fault-finding spirit	Compassionate, forgiving, look for the best in others
Independent, self-sufficient spirit	Dependent, recognize need for others
Maintain control, must be their way	Surrender control
Have to prove that they're right	Willing to yield the right to be right
Desire to be served	Motivated to serve others
Driven to be recognized / appreciated	Thrilled to be used at all; eager for others to get credit
Think of what they can do for God	Know that they have nothing to offer God
Feel confident in how much they know	Humbled by how much they have to learn
Defensive when criticized	Receive criticism with a humble, open heart
Find it difficult to share their spiritual needs with others	Willing to be open and transparent with others
Have a hard time saying, "I was wrong, will you please forgive me?"	Quick to admit failure and seek forgiveness
When there is a misunderstanding or conflict, waits for others to come and ask for forgiveness	Takes the initiative to be reconciled; see if they can get to the cross first

The "Servant Leader" must show his/her integrity in every area of life: faithfulness, (1 Cor. 4:1, 2; Col. 1:7; 4:7; 2 Tim. 22) and trustworthiness (Titus 1:7-9). The leader has to be an example to the followers as well as to family members, because followers want to know they can trust their leader. And the leader who can be trusted is the one who is faithful in every area of life. That's why moral purity in the life of a Servant leader is an essential part of integrity and trustworthiness.

The spiritual leader commands respect by virtue of his character not his/her position (1 Tim. 3:1-7; Titus 1:5-9; 1 Pet. 5:3). The leader should learn to create trust in others by complete honesty in all things. These four actions are practical and effective to create truthfulness; behave predictably and consistently; communicate clearly; treat promises seriously; and be forthright and candid. (1)

> *"Leadership is the capacity and will to rally men and women to a common purpose, and the character which inspires confidence."* ~Lord Montgomery

> *"A leader is one who recruits people to follow his example and effectively guides them along the way in accomplishing their objectives while he is training them to do what he does"*
> ~Myron Rush

> *"True leadership means to receive power from God and to use it under God's rule to serve people in God's way."*
> ~Leighton Ford

CALLING & GIFTING – INSTRUCTOR & INTERN, MENTOR & MENTEE

A "Calling" is personal

A "calling" is very important: the person being mentored must be called by God! If there is no calling, there is a very slim chance the person being mentored is going to be fully successful in doing the job that is required. To have this calling there must be a lot of prayer on the part of both the person mentoring and the protégé.

Only God can make a spiritual leader. Being in an important position does not guarantee that one is an effective leader. Spiritual leadership is a thing of the Holy Spirit and is conferred by God.

If and when God calls you into ministry, regardless of the task, ask God to give you a verse(s). When hard or difficult times come, and believe me they will, you will have something to fall back on that will get you through whatever you are experiencing. You also need to realize that if God calls you, God will see you through it (1 Thessalonians 5:24).

God will go before us to prepare the way, be with us as we go, pick us up when we fall, and will also pick up all the pieces to keep us going.

The Holy Spirit confers Spiritual Leadership

- Diversity of Spiritual Gifts (1 Corinthians 12; Ephesians 4)
- Distributes to each as He wills (1 Corinthians 12:11)

Gifts are distributed for the Common Good

- Equip the saints - Work of ministry (Ephesians 4:12)

- Build up the body of Christ (Ephesians 4:12)

If there is no calling, surely this person will leave or burn out.

BURNOUT

What are the signs of impending burnout or exhaustion in a leader? As I mentioned in Part I, here are some of the signs of which to be aware:

- Start losing focus
- Start making bad decisions
- Attitude changes
- Become less effective in one or more areas
    - Home Life
    - Personal Life
    - Work Life

How to Counteract Burnout

When we were CEF missionaries in Finland I was working and traveling night and day and not spending the time I should be spending with family. I was putting too much time and effort on the "Mission," and forgetting that I also had a family to tend.

So, after some time, the Lord impressed on me to take some time and take a good hard walk into the woods where we lived and spend time with Him.

That is what I did and to this day I have no idea how long I was alone with the Lord Jesus pouring my heart out to Him. What He showed me was amazing.

I went back to my house and family, and I found my wife and children completely changed. But it was not they who had changed; it was I. I was the problem all along and God showed me a very important lesson that I have never forgotten.

Sometimes we get so wrapped up in ourselves that we lose sight of what is really important; to keep a healthy balance between family, Mission and personal free time to rest.

- Step back – Rest

A dear friend's pastor slowed his pace. Their church's budget increased over 1000% in three years!

- Schedule
    - Personal Time
    - Family Time
    - Rest

Many times, we do not do any of these because we think the work is too important; that we should focus only on the mission. Our mission will not be sustained if we do not take the time and keep in mind the points just mentioned.

As David reminds us in Psalm 103:14: *"For he knows what we are made of, remembering that we are dust."* Howard Hendricks adds, *"... And He knows that dust does not produce!"*

So, the bottom line is that you and I need to keep a good balance in our schedules between work and family life.

Find an Accountability Partner

- Meet regularly
- Someone outside of work – more objective

HERITAGE & LEGACY

Heritage and Legacy are two aspects of life which we discuss too little. In Christianity, we have a great Heritage, and the opportunity to build a great Legacy. Let's talk about personal heritage.

A Heritage is Received

Heritage isn't our actions as we live life. They have very little to do with heritage. Heritage is something that comes or belongs to one by reason of birth. It is something transmitted by or acquired from a predecessor, simply because of the family into which we were born.

> *"A good man leaves an inheritance to his grandchildren ..."*
> Proverbs 13:22 (NKJV)

A Spiritual Heritage is received from **saints who have gone before us.**

We really have no control over this. Some come from areas where the leaders have been committed to doing what God has called them to do. Many of these new people have received a spiritual inheritance that would be envied by many.

Despite this deep spiritual heritage, they did nothing to get this. It is there simply because they followed some great leaders. They stand on the shoulders of all those who have gone before them.

> *What happened to so many over the past years that caused them to not follow God's way?*

That is why I'm writing this!

If we were to stop here, it would be a bit of a bummer! "Yes, you're reading this, but only because you have been blessed!" Heritage is no guarantee, but legacy provides hope to all.

Legacy is something you Build

While heritage is something received, legacy is something you create. Legacy is what you do with the heritage you received and subsequently offer to those who follow.

Legacy is something that we will all have, one way or the other. You've heard the phrase, "The proof is in the pudding," Legacy is the long-term proof of our work. Legacy is the picture of you in the next generation.

You can build your Legacy while...

- Working in the office
- Walking to the coffee shop
- Preparing for formal training
- ... and at numerous other times and in other venues.

Scripture talks about a lifestyle of training and building a spiritual legacy into your life.

> *"Listen, Israel: The Lord our God, the Lord is one. Love the Lord your God with all your heart, with all your soul, and with all your strength. These words that I am giving you today are to be in your heart. Repeat them to your children. Talk about them when you sit in your house and when you walk along the road, when you lie down and when you get up."* Deuteronomy 6:4-7 (NKJV)

When volunteers come alongside, they need to see you loving God with all your heart in absolutely everything you do. I believe that is what leaders of the past have tried to do, regardless of imperfections; their times of ill behavior; their flashes of selfishness; or the mistakes that they have made along the way. You have been given the benefit of their attempts to live Godly lives.

Heritage & Legacy

I would like to caution all those who are following. Know this; nothing is static. The benefits of your Heritage can be lost, walked away from or despised.

Build a Legacy

Love God – Make this a priority

Let them see you loving God with your whole heart, every day with no conditions. When Jesus was asked what the greatest commandment was. He said:

> *"Jesus answered, 'The most important is Listen, Israel! The Lord our God, the Lord is one. Love the Lord your God with all your heart, with all your soul, with all your mind, and with all your strength. The second is, Love your neighbor as yourself. There is no other command greater than these.'"* Mark 12:29-31 (NKJV)

Life is not always going to be easy. There will be days that will be hard. Never let those days cause you to abandon your heritage or jeopardize your Legacy.

Let them see you loving each other.

Let them see you actively respecting each other. You are from different tribes; it is going to show sometimes – probably frequently. Never let frustration cause you to abandon your heritage or jeopardize your legacy.

Pay the Price – Invest in the time, effort, and love.

There is a cost to ensuring the legacy you hope for. Not everyone is willing to pay the price for it. A legacy can be maintained... but, even maintenance has a price. It will demand effort and investment to offer the next generation the blessings you have received.

Learn from the saints who have gone before

The task for us all – is to live the life that stands on the shoulders of those who have gone before, seeing farther than they did and drawing closer to God with integrity and authenticity. The greatest part of that task is to inspire. Those who follow will run to you with arms upstretched, pleading with you to lift them up higher, that they, too, may love God more fully and see farther and do better than you have ever done.

As Spiritual Servant-Leaders, we need to demonstrate true humility in our spirits, attitudes, and actions.

Endnote:

1. An adaptation of Nancy Leigh DeMoss, *"Proud Spirits and Humble Hearts"* [cited on May 8, 2015] Online: http://www.bethanycommunitychurch.org/resources/docs/215-.PDF, in E. J. Hwang's paper on leadership.

QUESTIONS:

1. What are your thoughts on the case study presented?
2. What does servant-leadership require?
3. What are the leadership building tests (by R E Thompson)?
4. What are the goals of developing leaders?
5. How is servant-leadership developed?
6. Compare internship vs. mentorship program.
7. Describe a good personal leadership development plan.
8. Compare calling vs. gifting.
9. Name signs of burnout, and how to counteract it.
10. How do heritage and legacy play out?

7

Challenges of Leadership

INTRODUCTION TO CHALLENGES OF LEADERSHIP

Programs versus People

In some instances, there is a big gap in the church or mission programs. There may be great training in both areas, but too often we focus on the **program** rather than on the **person**.

Focus on the Person, not the Program

If leaders are going to be developed, focus needs to be on the person; time spent with the person (sit where they sit) to be able to meet their needs and to develop them.

When God gets the mentor and the protégé where He wants them, fruit will be evident.

Sit where they sit

I was teaching in the Bible College in Moscow. I spent most of my spare time with the students (We went to the Circus, to see a Hockey game and went to see a Folk-dance presentation). During this time, the students wanted to see how I live outside of the classroom. Some would even ride the bus and the Metro to my stop to see how I would act in certain situations. You need to "sit where they sit," spend time with them to really get to know them.

A QUICK RECAP

The Goals of Developing Leaders

- Maturity through Change
    - *Are you willing to change?*
- Multiply Disciples
    - *Can you reach all the lost ones in your community by yourself?*
- Reach 1 more Person, 1 more Family, 1 more Community
    - *Is it worth your time and effort?*

Internship vs. Mentoring Program

INTERNSHIP	MENTORING PROGRAM
Typically, a formal program	Typically, informal program
Includes written assessments	No written assessments
"On the Job Training (OJT)"	Train as you work & do life together
Often a finite period	Intended to repeat example; propagation

SIGNS OF LACK OF INTERNSHIPS / MENTORING

There are long-term consequences to not having internships or mentoring programs.

Work stops when the Worker stops.

The Church has seen many turn away from their calling because they were never in an internship or had any mentoring. If no one has been mentoring an assistant to take his/her place, the area may find another leader to take the slot, but this is not typical.

Declining ministry opportunities

What happens now is the area is without a leader, and depending on how soon a leader can be found for this area, the work continues to deteriorate. Another potentially fine leader is found to fill the vacancy. If he/she does not have an internship or somebody to shadow, most likely, this person will leave after 2 to 5 years or sooner.

Fewer people reached with the Gospel

If the leader is not mentoring someone to take his or her place, when this person leaves, that activity or ministry stops unless we can get another leader to take it. It is very important that the leader has an assistant right from the beginning. This keeps the organization going when and if he/she leaves; children, especially, love continuity. THE BOTTOM LINE IS TO KEEP REACHING AND GROWING.

The leader should not be worried about his or her job. If this individual is called to minister in the organization, that person will know his or her place of authority. This is where, again, it is important to follow what the founder of Child Evangelism Fellowship, Jesse Irvin Overholtzer, started from the beginning: work ourselves out of a job (2 Timothy 2:2).

If the director or leader does not have an assistant, it will not be too many years before this person will become overworked to the point of having to leave the work because of declining health or too much to handle alone. If there is no calling, surely this person will leave.

SIGNS OF EFFECTIVE INTERNSHIPS & MENTORING

However, if the person with some internship stays, this person should have an assistant to begin the process all over again.

Workers are multiplying

This process can take 2 to 5 years or longer, and if not done correctly, the work suffers. However, if done correctly, the work will grow. This is what happened in Northern Virginia, but it took a good ten (10) years to establish a foundation. God then sent us two capable men who have been in the internship program... for years!... and we have needed everyone including myself to keep up with the growth.

- GNCs are multiplying
- Peoples' lives are changed

EXPECT CHALLENGES

Dependence on God

Sometimes in leadership, one needs to go through crises that only God can solve. I want to share two situations:

First: I had a situation one time where a certain ethnic group wanted to do ministry a certain way which was not according to the organization's policy, and I prayed about this for many months. Until finally I called my chairman and treasurer to the office, and we had a Pray & Plan meeting. We produced a plan to attend their meeting and explain everything in detail. When we went to the meeting and explained the policy one of the members said, "Wayne, I got it, give me about half an hour or so and let me explain what you just explained to me." He did this and the response was amazing! They enthused, "this is exactly what we want to happen." When we do God's work God's way, it always works out to His Glory! Praise His Holy Name! Since that very day there have been no more situations, and the work has gone on as it should.

Work-Family Balance

Sometimes we get so wrapped up in ourselves that we lose sight of what is vitally important and that is to keep a healthy balance between family, the mission and your personal free time to take a rest. The order should be God, family, ministry.

"3Ps Rule"

Another lesson I would like to share is how to work with your children raising them up and how to collaborate with your co-workers, this is for all to take note: I call this the "3Ps Rule". I learned this from one of my uncles. Every time I was around them, they were always such a happy family, so I asked him why? Here is what he told me:

- **Pray** together
- **Plan** together
- **Play** together

I have applied this plan for all our children, and still today they will call Mom and Dad to get input for what they are thinking of doing and sometimes ask us to pray with them.

It takes time and effort to continue to develop leaders. If you want to expand the work in your area, you need to develop others to take leadership positions because you cannot manage everything yourself. One can only do so much. I would rather train and develop ten (10) people to do the work than try to do the work of ten (10) people. That is what happened in Northern Virginia CEF, and it has been exciting to be a part of seeing what God can do to make this happen.

We need to always show honest and sincere appreciation at every opportunity to leaders, teachers/helpers, and our prayer supporters so that they feel important. *Because they are.*

Be an Encourager

I believe we can fill this gap if we focus more on encouraging and developing people into Servant Leaders.

The reason I believe this is because I have spent over 50 years working in CEF. I have seen how many leaders have strayed from following Mr. Overholtzer's mandate to a self-mandate, resulting in this gap. As a result, leader after leader has left the work. If we do not develop someone to take our place, then we leave a gap because one person cannot do it all.

Too often an individual has been criticized rather than encouraged. I have seen teacher after teacher with no confidence who always tells me, "I could not be a coordinator or teach my peers." Natural leadership qualities all too often lie dormant and undiscovered. If we look carefully, we should be able to detect leadership potential. Moreover, if we have it, we should cultivate it and use it for Christ's work.

Build confidence - Do not expect perfection

It is not the education that God is looking for, although that certainly is a plus, but God is looking for a person who is CALLED to reach the lost. God does not necessarily call the equipped, but always equips the called. (1 Thessalonians 5:24)

As I spent time with the teachers and the summer missionaries, they stepped up and became wonderful leaders.

***Progressively* give ...**

- More responsibility
- More opportunities

God wants to show how strong He really is, and the Church today needs young men and women of God who will step up and be counted. Also, realize that it is God, alone, Who appoints leaders. That is a wonderful thought!

We also need to heed the warning that if the leaders fail to guide their people towards the spiritual uplands, then surely the path to the lowlands will be well worn. People live and travel together; no one thrives alone.

QUESTIONS:

1. Where should the focus be?
2. Describe signs of *lack of* mentorship/internship.
3. Describe signs of *effective* internship/mentorship.

8

Out-of-the-Box Thinking

More than ever, we need to be thinking "out-of-the-box" if we are to continue reaching the unreached. There is a notable example in the Gospel of Mark where four men were thinking "out-of-the-box", to reach Jesus so that one of their own might be healed. Charles H. Spurgeon's devotional provides principles revealed by the story.

THE PARALYTIC & THE ROOF

(From C. H. Spurgeon's *Morning and Evening* devotional, Morning, September 7)

"And when they could not come nigh unto him for the press, they uncovered the roof where he was: and when they had broken it up, they let down the bed wherein the sick of the palsy lay." *Mark 2:4, Authorized (King James) Version*

Faith is full of inventions. The house was full, a crowd blocked up the door, but faith found a way of getting at the Lord and placing the palsied man before him. If we cannot get sinners where Jesus is by ordinary methods, we must use extraordinary ones. It seems, according to Luke 5:19, that a tiling had to be removed, which would make dust and cause a measure of danger to those below, but where the case is very urgent, we must not mind running some risks and shocking some proprieties. Jesus was there to heal, and therefore, fall what might, faith ventured all so that her poor paralyzed charge might have his sins forgiven. O that we had more daring faith among us! Cannot we, dear reader, seek it this morning for ourselves and for our fellow-workers, and will we not try to-day to perform some gallant act for the love of souls and the glory of the Lord.

The world is constantly inventing; genius serves all the purposes of human desire: cannot faith invent too, and reach by some new means the outcasts who lie perishing around us? It was the presence of Jesus which excited victorious courage in the four bearers of the palsied man: is not the Lord among us now? Have we seen his face for ourselves this morning? Have we felt his healing power in our own souls? If so, then through door, through window, or through roof, let us, breaking through all impediments, labor to bring poor souls to Jesus. All means are good and decorous when faith and love are truly set on winning souls. If hunger for bread can break through stone walls, surely hunger for souls is not to be hindered in its efforts. O Lord, make us quick to suggest methods of reaching thy poor sin-sick ones, and bold to carry them out at all hazards."

Oh, that we could think "out-of-the-box", to reach more lost souls! What was stated earlier bears repeating; I have seen how, in the past, many leaders have gone from following Mr. Overholtzer's mandate to a self-mandate resulting in this gap. And leader after leader has left the work. *If we do not develop someone to take our place, we leave because one person cannot do it all.*

MR. O'S MANDATE

- Train others.
- Multiply your workers; train others to teach others.
- Multiply your ministry.

THINKING "OUT-OF-THE-BOX"

One needs to think "out-of-the-box" if we are to reach "one more person, one more family, one more community". Since Covid-19 has come to this world and the United States, it is even more imperative that we start thinking "out-of-the-box."

One must be willing to change.

If we are not always learning and changing, we are going backwards.

QUESTIONS:

1. What biblical story here demonstrates thinking "outside the box"?
2. What is the pertinent application?
3. Do you ever think outside commonly accepted parameters?
4. How?

Appendix A – Additional Resources

The resources listed below, two with a summary of their contents, are highly recommended additional studies to facilitate personal change and godly leadership.

- **"Teachers That Touch Lives"** CEF Super Seminar
- **"The Victorious Life"** Bible study (Overholtzer 1971)
    - The Victorious Life Rests on Mighty Promises
    - The Victorious Life Depends upon Justification by Faith
    - The Victorious Life Embraces Mysteries, Principles and Decisions
    - The Victorious Life Sets the Standard for Christian Conduct
    - The Victorious Life Is a Fully Yielded Life
    - The Victorious Life Requires a Renewed Mind
    - The Victorious Life Affects Our Bodies
    - The Victorious Life Is Filled with the Fruit of the Spirit
    - The Victorious Life and God's Provision for Growth
    - The Victorious Life and Its Dangers
    - Conflicts in the Victorious Life
    - The Glories of the Victorious Life
- **"Dynamics of Christian Leadership"** CEF Super Seminar series
    - The Christian Worker
    - Qualities of an Effective Leader
    - Importance of Example in Leadership
    - Cost of Leadership
    - The Servant Leader
    - Learning to Lead in Love
    - Motivating Your Workers
    - Recruiting and Leading Volunteers
    - Working With a Team

www.ingramcontent.com/pod-product-compliance
Lightning Source LLC
Chambersburg PA
CBHW071832290426
44109CB00017B/1803